To KAREN

from
Bro. Fred A.

$ 9.25

84 TH
STREET

D0397594

The Best of Bill

AA Grapevine, Inc.

ISBN 0-933685-41-6

AA Preamble

Alcoholics Anonymous is a fellowship of men and women who share their experience, strength and hope with each other that they may solve their common problem and help others to recover from alcoholism.

The only requirement for membership is a desire to stop drinking.

There are no dues or fees for AA membership; we are self-supporting through our own contributions.

AA is not allied with any sect, denomination, politics, organization or institution; does not wish to engage in any controversy, neither endorses nor opposes any causes.

Our primary purpose is to stay sober and help other alcoholics to achieve sobriety.

God grant me the serenity

to accept the things

I cannot change,

courage to change

the things I can,

and wisdom to know

the difference.

Table of Contents

Foreword

In 1935, a nondrinking alcoholic stock-broker from New York convinced a hung-over alcoholic surgeon in Akron, Ohio, that he didn't have to drink anymore. From that historic meeting, a program of recovery for more than two million once hopeless alcoholics in more than 150 countries was to grow and flourish.

To encourage, inspire, and stay in touch with this growing and far-flung fellowship, which called itself Alcoholics Anonymous, co-founder Bill W. turned to the Grapevine, a magazine created in New York in 1944 by "six ink-stained wretches" as Bill once good-humoredly referred to the sober women who started it. Born to immediate and wide-spread acceptance, the new publication became "The International Monthly Journal of Alcoholics Anonymous."

An energetic and prolific writer, Bill W.

authored nearly 150 articles in the Grapevine. In its pages, he chronicled the events of AA's pioneer years, and out of that early, arduous process of trial and error, he derived the principles that would unite and sustain this extraordinary fellowship. Ranging over a wide variety of topics, from the basic principles of AA's Steps and Traditions to the personal search for "emotional sobriety," Bill's words hold meaning not only for AA members but for anyone on a spiritual quest.

In 1988, as a result of the many requests over the years for reprints of five of these articles — "Faith," "Fear," "Honesty," "Humility," and "Love" — a collection entitled *The Best of Bill* was compiled. The enduring popularity of this little booklet has prompted the current editors of the Grapevine to issue this handsome new gift edition. As a fitting complement to these inspiring reflections on the spiritual life, we have included Bill's classic essay *Why Alcoholics Anonymous Is Anonymous*.

FAITH

God as We Understand Him

April 1961

The phrase "God as we understand him" is perhaps the most important expression to be found in our whole AA vocabulary. Within the compass of these five significant words there can be included every kind and degree of faith, together with the positive assurance that each of us may choose his own. Scarcely less valuable to us are those supplemental expressions — "a higher power" and "a power greater than ourselves." For all who deny, or seriously doubt a deity, these frame an open door over whose threshold the unbeliever can take his first easy step into a reality hitherto unknown to him — the realm of faith.

In AA such breakthroughs are everyday events. They are all the more remarkable when we reflect that a working faith had once seemed an impossibility of the first magnitude to perhaps half of our present membership of over 300,000. To all these doubters has come the great discovery that as soon as they could cast their main dependence upon a "higher power" — even upon their own AA groups — they had turned that blind corner which had always kept the open highway from their view. From this time on — assuming they tried hard to practice the rest of the AA program with a relaxed and open mind — an ever deepening and broadening faith, a veritable gift, had invariably put in its sometimes unexpected and often mysterious appearance.

We much regret that these facts of AA life are not understood by the legion of alcoholics in the world around us. Any number of them are bedeviled by the dire conviction that if ever they go near AA they will be pressured to conform to some particular brand of faith or theology. They just don't realize that faith is never a necessity for AA membership; that sobriety can be achieved with an easily acceptable minimum of it; and that our concepts of a higher power and God as we understand him afford everyone a nearly unlimited choice of spiritual belief and action.

How to transmit this good news is one of our most challenging problems in communication, for which there may be no fast or sweeping answer. Perhaps our public information services could begin to emphasize this all-important aspect of AA more heavily. And within our own ranks we might well develop a more sympathetic awareness of the acute plight of these really isolated and desperate sufferers. In their aid we can settle for no less than the best possible attitude and the most ingenious action that we can muster.

We can also take a fresh look at the problem of "no faith" as it exists right on our own doorstep. Though 300,000 have recovered in the last twenty-five years, maybe half a million more have walked into our midst, and then out again. No doubt some were too sick to make even a start. Others couldn't or wouldn't admit their alcoholism. Still others couldn't face up to their underlying personality defects. Numbers departed for still other reasons.

Yet we can't well content ourselves with the view that all these recovery failures were entirely the fault of the newcomers themselves. Perhaps a great many didn't receive the kind and amount of sponsorship they so sorely needed. We didn't communicate when we might have done so. So we AAs failed them. Perhaps more often than we think, we still make no contact at depth with those suffering the dilemma of no faith.

Certainly none are more sensitive to spiritual cocksureness, pride, and aggression than they are. I'm sure this is something we too often forget. In AA's first years I all but ruined the whole undertaking with this sort of unconscious arrogance. God as *I* understood him *had* to be for everybody. Sometimes my aggression was subtle and sometimes it was crude. But either way it was damaging — perhaps fatally so — to numbers of non-believers. Of course this sort of thing isn't confined to Twelfth Step work. It is very apt to leak out into our relations with everybody. Even now, I catch myself chanting that same old barrier-building refrain, "Do as *I* do, believe as *I* do — or else!"

Here's a recent example of the high cost of spiritual pride. A very tough-minded prospect was taken to his first AA meeting. The first speaker majored on his own drinking pattern. The prospect seemed impressed. The next two speakers (or maybe lecturers) each themed their talks on "God as *I* understand him." This could have been good, too, but it certainly wasn't. The trouble was their attitude, the way they presented their experience. They did ooze arrogance. In fact, the final speaker got far overboard on some of his personal theological convictions. With perfect fidelity, both were repeating my performance of years before. Quite unspoken, yet implicit in everything they said, was the same idea — "Folks, listen to us. We have the only true brand of AA — and you'd better get it!"

The new prospect said he'd had it — and he had. His sponsor protested that this wasn't real AA. But it was too late; nobody could touch him after that. He also had a first class alibi for yet another bender. When last heard from, an early appointment with the undertaker seemed probable.

Fortunately, such rank aggression in the name of spirituality isn't often seen nowadays. Yet this sorry and unusual episode can be turned to good account. We can ask ourselves whether, in less obvious but nevertheless destructive forms, we are not more subject to fits of spiritual pride than we had supposed. If constantly worked at, I'm sure that no kind of self-survey could be more beneficial. Nothing could more surely increase our communication with each other and with God.

Many years ago a so-called unbeliever brought me to see this very clearly. He was an M.D. and a fine one. I met him and his wife Mary at the home of a friend in a Midwestern city. It was purely a social evening. Our Fellowship of alcoholics was my sole topic and I pretty much monopolized the conversation. Nevertheless, the doctor and his lady seemed truly interested and he asked many questions. But one of them made me suspect that he was an agnostic, or maybe an atheist.

This promptly triggered me, and I set out to convert him, then and there. Deadly serious, I actually bragged about my spectacular spiritual experience of the year before. The doctor mildly wondered if that experience might not be something other than I thought it was. This hit me hard, and I was downright rude. There had been no real provocation; the doctor was uniformly courteous, good-humored, and even respectful. Not a little wistfully, he said he often wished he had a firm faith, too. But plainly enough, I had convinced him of nothing.

Three years later I revisited my Midwestern friend. Mary, the doctor's wife, came by for a call and I learned that he had died the week before. Much affected, she began to speak of him.

His was a noted Boston family, and he'd been Harvard educated. A brilliant student, he might have gone on to fame in his profession. He could have enjoyed a wealthy practice and a social life among old friends. Instead, he had insisted on being a company doctor in what was a strife-torn industrial town. When Mary had sometimes asked why they didn't go back to Boston, he would take her hand and say, "Maybe you are right, but I can't bring myself to leave. I think the people at the company really need me."

Mary then recalled that she had never known her husband to complain seriously about anything, or to criticize anyone bitterly. Though he appeared to be perfectly well, the doctor had slowed down in his last five years. When Mary prodded him to go out evenings, or tried to get him to the office on time, he always came up with a plausible and good-natured excuse. Not until his sudden last illness did she know that all this while he had carried about a heart condition that could have done him in at any moment. Except for a single doctor on his own staff, no one had an inkling. When she reproached him about this, he simply said, "Well, I could see no good in causing people to worry about me — especially you, my dear."

This was the story of a man of great spiritual worth. The hallmarks were plain to be seen: humor and patience, gentleness and courage, humility and dedication, unselfishness and love — a demonstration I might never come near to making myself. This was the man I had chided and patronized. This was the "unbeliever" I had presumed to instruct!

Mary told us this story more than twenty

years ago. Then, for the first time, it burst in upon me how very dead faith can be — when minus responsibility. The doctor had an unwavering belief in his ideals. But he also practiced humility, wisdom, and responsibility. Hence his superb demonstration.

My own spiritual awakening had given me a built-in faith in God — a gift indeed. But I had been neither humble nor wise. Boasting of my faith, I had forgotten my ideals. Pride and irresponsibility had taken their place. By so cutting off my own light, I had little to offer my fellow alcoholics. Therefore my faith was dead to them. At last I saw why many had gone away — some of them forever.

Therefore, faith is more than our greatest gift; its sharing with others is our greatest responsibility. So may we of AA continually seek the wisdom and the willingness by which we may well fulfill that immense trust which the giver of all perfect gifts has placed in our hands.

This Matter of

FEAR

January 1962

As the AA Book says, "Fear is an evil, corroding thread; the fabric of our lives is shot through with it." Fear is surely a bar to reason, and to love, and of course it invariably powers anger, vainglory, and aggression. It underlies maudlin guilt and paralyzing depression. President Roosevelt once made the significant remark that "We have nothing to fear but fear itself."

This is a severe indictment, and it is possibly too sweeping. For all its usual destructiveness, we have found that fear can be the starting point for better things. Fear can be a stepping stone to prudence and to a decent respect for others. It can point the path to justice, as well as to hate. And the more we have of respect and justice, the more we shall begin to find the love which can suffer much, and yet be freely given. So fear need not always be destructive, because the lessons of its consequences can lead us to positive values.

The achievement of freedom from fear is a lifetime undertaking, one that can never be wholly completed. When under heavy attack, acute illness, or in other conditions of serious insecurity, we shall all react, well or badly, as the case may be. Only the vainglorious claim perfect freedom from fear, though their very grandiosity is really rooted in the fears they have temporarily forgotten.

Therefore the problem of resolving fear has two aspects. We shall have to try for all the freedom from fear that is possible for us to attain. Then we shall need to find both the courage and the grace to deal constructively with whatever fears remain. Trying to understand our fears, and the fears of others, is but a first step. The larger question is how, and where, we go from there.

Since AA's beginning, I have watched as thousands of my fellows became more and more able to understand and to transcend their fears. These examples have been of unfailing help and inspiration. Perhaps, then, some of my own experiences with fear and the shedding of it to an encouraging degree may be appropriate.

As a child, I had some pretty heavy emotional shocks. There was deep family disturbance; I was physically awkward and the like. Of course other kids have such emotional handicaps and emerge unscathed. But I didn't. Evidently I was over-sensitive, and therefore over-scared. Anyhow, I developed a positive phobia that I wasn't like other youngsters, and never could be. At first this threw me into depression and thence into the isolation of retreat.

But these child miseries, all of them generated by fear, became so unbearable that I turned highly aggressive. Thinking I never could belong, and vowing I'd never settle for any second-rate status, I felt I simply had to dominate in everything I chose to do, work or play. As this attractive formula for the good life began to succeed, according to my then specifications of success, I became deliriously happy. But when an undertaking occasionally did fail, I was filled with a resentment and depression that could be cured only by the next triumph. Very early, therefore, I came to value everything in terms of victory or defeat — all or nothing. The only satisfaction I knew was to win.

This was my false antidote for fear and this was the pattern, ever more deeply etched, that dogged me through school days, World War I, the hectic drinking career in Wall Street, and down into the final hour of my complete collapse. By that time adversity was no longer a stimulant, and I knew not whether my greater fear was to live or to die.

While my basic fear pattern is a very common one, there are of course many others. Indeed, fear manifestations and the problems that trail in their wake are so numerous and complex that in this brief article it is not possible to detail even a few of them. We can only review those spiritual resources and principles by which we may be able to face and deal with fear in any of its aspects.

In my own case, the foundation stone of freedom from fear is that of faith: a faith that, despite all worldly appearances to the contrary, causes me to believe that I live in a universe that makes sense. To me, this means a belief in a Creator who is all power, justice, and love; a God who intends for me a purpose, a meaning and a destiny to grow, however little and halting, toward his own likeness and image. Before the coming of faith I had lived as an alien in a cosmos that too often seemed both hostile and cruel. In it there could be no inner security for me.

Dr. Carl Jung, one of the three founders of modern depth psychology, had a profound conviction upon this great dilemma of the world today. In paraphrase, this is what he had to say about it: "Any person who has reached forty years of age, and who still has no means of comprehending who he is, where he is, or where he is next going, cannot avoid becoming a neurotic — to some degree or other. This is true whether his youthful drives for sex, material security, and a place in society have been satisfied, or not satisfied." When the benign doctor said "becoming neurotic" he might just as well have said "becoming fear-ridden."

This is exactly why we of AA place such emphasis on the need for faith in a higher power, define that as we may. We have to find a life in the world of grace and spirit, and this is certainly a new dimension for most of us. Surprisingly, our quest for this realm of being is not too difficult. Our conscious entry into it usually begins as soon as we have deeply confessed our personal powerlessness to go on alone, and have made our appeal to whatever

God we think there is — or may be. The gift of faith and the consciousness of a higher power is the outcome. As faith grows, so does inner security. The vast underlying fear of nothingness commences to subside. Therefore we of AA find that our basic antidote for fear is a spiritual awakening.

It so happens that my own spiritual perception was electrically sudden and absolutely convincing. At once I became a part — if only a tiny part — of a cosmos that was ruled by justice and love in the person of God. No matter what had been the consequences of my own willfulness and ignorance, or those of my fellow travelers on earth, this was still the truth. Such was the new and positive assurance, and this has never left me. I was given to know, at least for the time being, what the absence of fear could be like. Of course my own gift of faith is not essentially different from those spiritual awakenings since received by countless AAs — it was only more sudden. But even this new frame of reference

— critically important though it was — only marked my entrance into that long path which leads away from fear, and toward love. The old and deeply carved etchings of anxiety were not instantly and permanently rubbed out. Of course they reappeared, and sometimes alarmingly.

Being the recipient of such a spectacular spiritual experience, it was not surprising that the first phase of my AA life was characterized by a great deal of pride and power-driving. The craving for influence and approval, the desire to be *the* leader was still very much with me. Better still, this behavior could now be justified — all in the name of good works!

It fortunately turned out that this rather blatant phase of my grandiosity, which lasted some years, was followed by a string of adversities. My demands for approval, which were obviously based on the fear that I might not get enough of it, began to collide with these identical traits in my fellow AAs. Hence their saving of the Fellowship from me, and I saving it from them, became an all-absorbing occupation. This of course resulted in anger, suspicion, and all sorts of frightening episodes. In this remarkable and now rather amusing era of our affairs, any number of us commenced playing God all over again. For some years AA power-drivers ran hog-wild. But out of this fearsome situation, the Twelve Steps and the Twelve Traditions of AA were formulated. Mainly these were principles designed for ego reduction, and therefore for the reduction of our fears. These were the principles which we hoped would hold us in unity and increasing love for each other and for God.

Gradually we began to be able to accept the other fellow's sins as well as his virtues. It was in this period that we coined the potent and meaningful expression, "Let us always love the best in others — and never fear their worst." After some ten years of trying to work this brand of love and the ego-reducing properties of the AA Steps and Traditions into the life of our society, the awful fears for the survival of AA simply vanished.

The practice of AA's Twelve Steps and Twelve Traditions in our personal lives also brought incredible releases from fear of every description, despite the wide prevalence of formidable personal problems. When fear did persist, we knew it for what it was, and under God's grace we became able to handle it. We began to see each adversity as a God-given opportunity to develop the kind of courage which is born of humility, rather than of bravado. Thus we were enabled to accept ourselves, our circumstances, and our fellows. Under God's grace we even found that we could die with decency, dignity, and faith, knowing that "the Father doeth the works."

We of AA now find ourselves living in a world characterized by destructive fears as never before in history. But in it we nevertheless see great areas of faith and tremendous aspirations toward justice and brotherhood. Yet no prophet can presume to say whether the world outcome will be blazing destruction or the beginning, under God's intention, of the brightest era yet known to mankind. I am sure we AAs well comprehend this scene. In microcosm, we have experienced this identical state of terrifying uncertainty, each in his own life. In no sense pridefully, we AAs can say that we do not fear the world outcome, whichever course it may take. This is because we have been enabled to deeply feel and say, "We shall fear no evil — thy will, not ours, be done."

Often told, the following story can nevertheless bear repeating. On the day that the staggering calamity of Pearl Harbor fell upon our country, a friend of AA, and one of the greatest spiritual figures that we may ever know, was walking along a street in St. Louis. This was, of course, our well-loved Father Edward Dowling of the Jesuit Order. Though not an alcoholic, he had been one of the founders and a prime inspiration of the struggling AA group in his city. Because large numbers of his usually sober friends had already taken to their bottles that they might blot out the implications of the Pearl Harbor disaster, Father Ed was understandably anguished by the probability that his cherished AA group would scarcely settle for less. To Father Ed's mind, this would be a first-class calamity, all of itself.

Then an AA member, sober less than a year, stepped alongside and engaged Father Ed in a spirited conversation — mostly about AA. As Father Ed saw, with relief, his companion was perfectly sober. And not a word did he volunteer about the Pearl Harbor business.

Wondering happily about this, the good father queried, "How is it that you have nothing to say about Pearl Harbor? How can you roll with a punch like that?"

"Well," replied the AA, "I'm really surprised that you don't know. Each and every one of us in AA has already had his own private Pearl Harbor. So, I ask you, why should we alcoholics crack up over this one?"

This Matter of

HONESTY

August 1961

The problem of honesty touches nearly every aspect of our lives. There are, for example, the widespread and amazing phenomena of self-deception. There are those rather dreadful brands of reckless truth-telling, which are so often lacking in prudence and love. Then there are those countless life situations in which nothing less than utter honesty will do, no matter how sorely we may be tempted by the fear and pride that would reduce us to half-truths or inexcusable denials.

Let's first see what self-deception can do to one's integrity.

Well remembered is the comfort I used to take from an exaggerated belief in my own honesty. My New England kinsfolk had thoroughly taught me the sanctity of all business commitments and contracts. They insisted that "a man's word is his bond." I delighted in the Lincoln story which tells how Honest Abe once walked six miles to return the six pennies he had overcharged a poor woman at his grocery. After this rigorous conditioning, business honesty always came easy, and it stayed with me. Even in Wall Street, where I landed years later, I never flim-flammed anyone.

However, this small fragment of easy-won virtue did produce some interesting liabilities. I was so absurdly proud of my business standards that I never failed to whip up a fine contempt for those of my fellow Wall Streeters who were prone to short-change their customers. This was arrogant enough, but the ensuing self-deception proved even worse. My prized business honesty was presently converted into a comfortable cloak under which I could hide the many serious flaws that beset other departments of my life. Being certain of this one virtue, it was easy to conclude that I had them all. For years on end, this prevented me from taking a good look at myself. This is a very ordinary example of the fabulous capacity for self-deception that nearly all of us can display at times. Moreover, the deception of others is nearly always rooted in the deception of ourselves.

As further illustrations, two extreme cases come to mind. One shows self-delusion in a very obvious form — obvious, that is, to all but the victim himself. The other depicts the more subtle brand of self-delusion, from which no human being can be entirely exempt.

One of my good friends used to be a safe-cracker. He told me this revealing tale. Said he: "You know, Bill, I used to think I was a kind of one-man revolution against society. All over the world I could see the 'have-nots' taking it away from the 'haves.' This seemed very reasonable. After all, those damn 'haves' just wouldn't share their wealth. The revolutions that took it away from them were apt to get a lot of applause. But guys like me, who could also make those 'haves' share their wealth, got no such glad hand. After a while I figured this out: the plain fact was that nobody liked burglars. Revolutions, yes — but burglars, no. Anyway, I couldn't see anything wrong about blowing safes, excepting getting caught. Even after years in jail, I still couldn't see it. When AA showed up, I slowly began to get it through my head that there were good revolutions and bad ones. Bit by bit it dawned on me how I'd completely fooled myself. I could see that I had been pretty crazy. How I could have been *that* dumb, I'll never be able to explain in any other way."

Now I have another AA friend, a good and gentle soul. He recently joined one of the great religious orders, one in which the friars spend many hours a day in contemplation. So my friend has plenty of time to take his inventory. The more he looks, the more unconscious self-deception he finds. And the more astonished he becomes at the elaborate and devious excuse-making machinery by which he had been justifying himself. He has already come to the conclusion that the prideful righteousness of "good people" may often be just as destructive as the glaring sins of those who are supposedly not so good. So he daily looks inward upon himself and then upward toward God, the better to discover just where he stands in this matter of honesty. Out of each of his meditations there always emerges one dead certainty, and this is the fact that he still has a long way to go.

Just how and when we tell the truth — or keep silent — can often reveal the differences between genuine integrity and none at all. Step Nine of AA's program emphatically cautions us against misusing the truth when it states: "Made direct amends to such people wherever possible, except when to do so would injure them or others." Because it points up the fact that the truth can be used to injure as well as to heal, this valuable principle certainly has a wide-ranging application to the problem of developing integrity.

In AA, for instance, we talk a great deal about each other. Provided our motives are thoroughly good, this is not in the least wrong. But damaging gossip is quite something else. Of course, this kind of scuttlebutt can be well grounded in fact. But no such abuse of the facts could ever be twisted into anything resembling integrity. It can't be maintained that this sort of superficial honesty is good for anyone. So the need to examine ourselves is very much with us. Following a gossip binge we can well ask ourselves these questions: "Why did we say what we did? Were we only trying to be helpful and informative? Or were we not trying to feel superior by confessing the other fellow's sins? Or, because of fear and dislike, were we not really aiming to damage him?" This would be an honest attempt to examine ourselves, rather than the other fellow. Here we see the difference between the use of the truth and its misuse. Right here we begin to regain the integrity we had lost.

Sometimes, though, our true motives are not so easily determined. There are times when we think we must reveal highly damaging facts so that we may stop the depredations of certain evil-doers. "All for the good of AA" — or what have you — now becomes our cry. Armed with this often false justification, we righteously press our attack. True enough, there may be a genuine need to remedy a damaging condition. True enough, we may have to make use of some unpleasant facts. But the real test is how we handle ourselves. We must be ever so certain that we are not pots who call the kettles black. Therefore it is wise if we pose ourselves these questions: "Do we really understand the people who are involved in this situation? Are we certain that we have *all* of the facts? Is any action or criticism on our part really necessary? Are we positive that we are neither fearful nor angry?" Only following such a scrutiny can we be sure to act with the careful discrimination and in the loving spirit that will always be needed to maintain our own integrity.

Now here is another aspect of the honesty problem. It is very possible for us to use the alleged dishonesty of other people as a most plausible excuse for not meeting our own obligations. I once had a spell of this myself. Some rather prejudiced friends had exhorted me never to go back to Wall Street. They were sure that the rampant materialism and double-dealing down there would be sure to stunt my spiritual growth. Because this sounded so high-minded, I continued to stay away from the only business that I knew.

When finally my household went quite broke, I woke up to the fact that I hadn't been able to face the prospect of going back to work. So I returned to Wall Street after all. And I have ever since been glad that I did. I needed to rediscover that there are many fine people in New York's financial district. Then, too, I needed the experience of staying sober in the very surroundings where alcohol had cut me down. I did receive all these benefits and a great deal more. Indeed, there was one colossal dividend that resulted directly from my grudging decision to re-enter the market place. It was a Wall Street business trip to Akron, Ohio, in 1935, that first brought me face to face with Dr. Bob — AA's co-founder-to-be. So the birth of AA itself actually hinged on the fact that I had been trying to meet my bread-and-butter responsibilities.

We must now leave the absorbing topic of self-delusion and look at some of those trying life situations which we have to meet foursquare and head-on. Suppose we are handed an employment application that asks, "Have you ever suffered from alcoholism, and were you ever hospitalized?" Here, we AAs can assuredly make a good report of ourselves. Almost to a man we believe that nothing short of the absolute truth will do in situations of this type. Most employers respect our Fellowship and they like this rugged brand of honesty, especially when we reveal our AA membership and its results. Of course many another life problem calls for this identical brand of forthrightness. For the most part, situations requiring utter honesty are clear-cut, and readily recognizable. We simply have to face up to them, our fear and pride regardless. Failing to do this, we shall be sure to suffer those ever mounting conflicts which can only be resolved by plain honesty.

There are, nevertheless, certain occasions where reckless truth-telling may create widespread havoc and permanent damage to others. Whenever this seems possible, we are likely to find ourselves in a bad jam indeed. We shall be torn between two temptations. When conscience agonizes us enough, we may well cast all prudence and love to the winds. We may try to buy our freedom by telling the brutal truth, no matter who gets hurt or how much. But this is not the usual temptation. It is far more probable that we shall veer to the other extreme. We will paint for ourselves a most unrealistic picture of the awful damage we are about to inflict on others. By claiming great compassion and love for our supposed victims, we are getting set to tell the Big Lie — and be thoroughly comfortable about it, too.

When life presents us with a racking conflict like this, we cannot be altogether blamed if we are confused. In fact, our very first responsibility is to admit that we *are* confused. We may have to confess that, for the time being, we have lost all ability to tell right from wrong. Most difficult, too, will be the admission that we cannot be certain of receiving God's guidance because our prayers are so cluttered with wishful thinking. Surely this is the point at which we must seek the counsel of our finest friends. There is nowhere else to go.

33

Had I not been blessed with wise and loving advisers, I might have cracked up long ago. A doctor once saved me from death by alcoholism because he obliged me to face up to the deadliness of that malady. Another doctor, a psychiatrist, later on helped me save my sanity because he led me to ferret out some of my deep-lying defects. From a clergyman I acquired the truthful principles by which we AAs now try to live. But these precious friends did far more than supply me with their professional skills. I learned that I could go to them with any problem whatever. Their wisdom and their integrity were mine for the asking. Many of my dearest AA friends have stood with me in exactly this same relation. Oftentimes they could help where others could not, simply because they *were* AAs.

Of course we cannot wholly rely on friends to solve all our difficulties. A good advisor will never do all our thinking for us. He knows that each final choice must be ours.

He will therefore help to eliminate fear, expediency, and self-deception, so enabling us to make choices which are loving, wise, and honest.

The choice of such a friend is an all-important matter. We should look for a person of deep understanding, and then carefully listen to what he has to say. In addition, we must be positive that our prospective adviser will hold our communications in the strictest of confidence. Should he be a clergyman or doctor or lawyer, this can be taken for granted. But when we consult an AA friend, we should not be reluctant to remind him of our need for full privacy. Intimate communication is normally so free and easy among us that an AA adviser may sometimes forget when we expect him to remain silent. The protective sanctity of this most healing of human relations ought never be violated.

Such privileged communications have priceless advantages. We find in them the perfect opportunity to be as honest as we know how to be. We do not have to think of the possibility of damage to other people, nor need we fear ridicule or condemnation. Here, too, we have the best possible chance of spotting self-deception.

If we are fooling ourselves, a competent adviser can see this quickly. And, as he guides us out of our fantasies, we are surprised to find that we have few of the usual urges to defend ourselves against unpleasant truths. In no other way can fear, pride, and ignorance be so readily melted. After a time, we realize the we are standing firm on a brand-new foundation for integrity.

Let us therefore continue our several searches for self-deception, great or small. Let us painstakingly temper honesty with prudence and love. And let us never flinch from entire forthrightness whenever this is the requirement.

How truth makes us free is something that we AAs can well understand. It cut the shackles that once bonded us to alcohol. It continues to release us from conflicts and miseries beyond reckoning; it banishes fear and isolation. The unity of our Fellowship, the love we cherish for each other, the esteem in which the world holds us — all of these are products of such integrity as, under God, we have been privileged to achieve. May we therefore quicken our search for still more genuine honesty and deepen its practice in all our affairs.

HUMILITY

for Today

June 1961

There can be no absolute humility for us humans. At best, we can only glimpse the meaning and splendor of such a perfect ideal. As the book *Alcoholics Anonymous* says: "We are not saints ... we claim spiritual progress rather than spiritual perfection." Only God himself can manifest in the absolute; we human beings must needs live and grow in the domain of the relative. We seek humility for today.

Therefore our practical question is this: "Just what do we mean by 'humility for today' and how do we know when we have found it?"

We scarcely need be reminded that excessive guilt or rebellion leads to spiritual poverty. But it was a very long time before we knew we could go even more broke on spiritual pride. When we early AAs got our first glimmer of how spiritually prideful we could be, we coined this expression: "Don't try to get too damned good by Thursday!" That old-time admonition may look like another of those handy alibis that can excuse us from trying for our best. Yet a closer view reveals just the contrary. This is our AA way of warning against pride-blindness, and the imaginary perfections that we do not possess.

Now that we no longer patronize bars and bordellos; now that we bring home the paychecks; now that we are so very active in AA; and now that people congratulate us on these signs of progress — well, we naturally proceed to congratulate ourselves. Yet we may not be within hailing distance of humility. Meaning well, yet doing badly, how often have I said or thought, "I am right and you are wrong," "My plan is correct and yours is faulty," "Thank God your sins are not my sins," "You are hurting AA and I'm going to stop you cold," "I have God's guidance, so he is on my side." And so on, indefinitely.

The alarming thing about such pride-blindness is the ease with which it is justified. But we need not look far to see that this deceptive brand of self-justification is a universal destroyer of harmony and of love. It sets person against person, nation against nation. By it, every form of folly and violence can be made to look right, and even respectable. Of course it is not for us to condemn. We need only investigate ourselves.

How, then, can we do more and more about reducing our guilt, rebellion, and pride?

When I inventory such defects, I like to draw a picture and tell myself a story. My picture is that of a Highway to Humility, and my story is an allegory. On one side of my Highway, I see a great bog. The Highway's edge borders a shallow marsh which finally shelves down into that muddy morass of guilt and rebellion in which I have so often floundered. Self-destruction lies in wait out there, and I know this. But the country on the other side of the road looks fine. I see inviting glades, and beyond them great mountains. The countless trails leading into this pleasant land look safe. It will be easy, I think, to find one's way back.

Together with numbers of friends, I decide to take a brief detour. We pick our path and happily plunge along it. Elatedly, somebody soon says, "Maybe we'll find gold on top of that mountain." Then to our amazement we do strike gold — not nuggets in the streams, but fully minted coins. The heads of these coins each declare, "This is pure gold — twenty-four carats." Surely, we think, this is the reward for our patient plodding back there in the everlasting brightness of the Highway.

Soon, though, we begin to notice the words on the tails of our coins, and we have strange forebodings: Some pieces carry rather attractive inscriptions. "I am Power," "I am Acclaim," "I am Wealth," "I am Righteousness," they say. But others seem very strange. For example: "I am the Master Race," "I am the Benefactor," "I am Good Causes," "I am God." This is very puzzling. Nevertheless we pocket them. But next come real shockers. They read: "I'm Pride," "I'm Revenge," "I'm Disunity," "I'm Chaos." Then we turn up a single coin — just one — which declares: "I am the Devil himself." Some of us are horrified and we cry, "This is fool's gold, and this is a fool's paradise — let's clear out of here!"

But many would not return with us. They said, "Let's stay here and sort over those damned coins. We'll pick only the ones that carry the lucky inscriptions. For instance, those that say, 'Power' and 'Glory' and 'Righteousness.' You fellows are going to be sorry you didn't stick around." Not strangely, it was years before this part of our original company returned to the Highway.

They told us the story of those who had

sworn never to return. They had said, "This money is real gold, and don't tell us any different. We're going to pile up all we can. Sure, we don't like those fool mottoes. But there's plenty of firewood here. We'll just melt all this stuff down into good solid gold bricks." Then our late arrivals added: "This is how the gold of Pride claimed our brothers. They were already quarreling over their bricks when we left. Some were hurt and a few were dying. They had begun to destroy each other."

This symbolic picture graphically tells me that I may attain "humility for today" only to the extent that I am able to avoid the bog of guilt and rebellion, and that fair but deceiving land which is strewn with the coin of Pride. This is how I can find and stay on the Road to Humility which lies in between. Therefore, a constant inventory which can reveal when I am off the road is always in order.

Of course, our first attempts at such inventories are apt to prove very unrealistic. I used to be a champ at *unrealistic* self-appraisal. I wanted to look only at the part of my life which seemed good. Then I would greatly exaggerate whatever virtues I supposed I had attained. Next I would congratulate myself on the grand job I was doing. So my unconscious self-deception never failed to turn my few good assets into serious liabilities. This astonishing process was always a pleasant one. Naturally this generated a terrible hankering for still more "accomplishments," and still more approval. I was falling straight back into the pattern of my drinking days. Here were the same old goals — power, fame, and applause. Besides, I had the best alibi known — the spiritual alibi. The fact that I really did have a spiritual objective always made this utter nonsense seem perfectly right. I couldn't tell a good coin from a bad one; it was spiritual gold-bricking at its worst. I shall forever regret the damage I did to people around me. Indeed, I still tremble when I realize what I might have done to AA and to its future.

In those days I wasn't much bothered about

the areas of life in which I was standing still. There was always the alibi. "After all," I said to myself, "I'm far too busy with much more important matters." That was my near perfect prescription for comfort and complacency.

But sometimes I would simply have to look at certain situations where, on the face of them, I was doing very badly. Right away, a rousing rebellion would set in. Then the search for excuses would become frantic. "These," I would exclaim, "are really a good man's faults." When that pet gadget finally broke apart, I would think, "Well, if those people would only treat me right, I wouldn't have to behave the way I do." Next in order was this: "God well knows that I do have *awful compulsions*. I just can't get over this one. So *he* will have to release me." At last came the time when I would shout, "*This*, I positively *will not do*; I *won't even try*." Of course my conflicts went right on mounting because I was simply loaded with excuses and refusals.

When these troubles had finally exhausted

45

me enough, there was yet another escape. I would commence to wallow in the bog of guilt. Here pride and rebellion would give way to depression. Though the variations were many, my main theme always was, "How god-awful I am." Just as I had exaggerated my modest attainments by pride, so now I would exaggerate my defects through guilt. I would race about, confessing all (and a great deal more!) to whoever would listen. Believe it or not, I took that to be great humility on my part, and I counted this as my sole remaining asset and consolation!

During those bouts with guilt, there was never a decent regret for the harms I had done, nor was there any serious thought of making such restitution as I could. The idea of asking God's forgiveness, let alone any forgiveness of myself, never occurred to me. Of course my really big liability — spiritual pride and arrogance — was not examined at all. I had shut out the light by which I might have seen it.

Today I think I can trace a clear linkage between my guilt and my pride. Both of them were certainly attention-getters. In pride I could say, "Look at me, I am wonderful." In guilt I would moan, "I'm awful." Therefore guilt is really the reverse side of the coin of pride. Guilt aims at self-destruction, and pride aims at the destruction of others.

This is why I see humility for today as that safe and secure stance midway between these violent emotional extremes. It is a quiet place where I can keep enough perspective, and enough balance, to take my next small step up the clearly marked road that points toward eternal values.

Many of us have experienced far greater emotional gyrations than I. Others have experienced less. But all of us still have them at times. Yet I think we need not regret these conflicts. They seem to be a necessary part of growing up, emotionally and spiritually. They are the raw material out of which much of our progress has to be made.

Does anyone ask if AA is but a retching

pit of pain and conflict? The answer is "Certainly not." In great measure, we AAs have really found peace. However haltingly, we have managed to attain an increasing humility whose dividends have been serenity and legitimate joy. We do not detour as much or as far as we once did.

At the outset of this meditation, it was thought that absolute ideals are far beyond our attainment, or even our comprehension; that we would be sadly lacking in humility if we really felt that we could achieve anything like absolute perfection in this brief span of earthly existence. Such a presumption would certainly be the acme of spiritual pride.

Reasoning thus, many people will have no truck at all with absolute spiritual values. Perfectionists, they say, are either full of conceit because they fancy they have reached some impossible goal, or else they are swamped in self-condemnation because they have not done so.

Yet I think that we should not hold this

view. It is not the fault of great ideals that they are sometimes misused and so become shallow excuses for guilt, rebellion, and pride. On the contrary, we cannot grow very much unless we constantly try to envision what the eternal spiritual values are. As Step Eleven of AA's recovery program says, we "Sought through prayer and meditation to improve our conscious contact with God as we understood him, praying only for knowledge of his will for us and the power to carry that out." This surely means that we ought to look toward God's perfection as our guide rather than as a goal to be reached in any foreseeable time.

I'm sure, for instance, that I ought to seek out the finest definition of humility that is possible for me to envision. This definition doesn't have to be absolutely perfect — I am only asked to try. Suppose I choose one like this: "Perfect humility would be a state of complete freedom from myself, freedom from all the claims that my defects of character now lay so heavily upon me. Perfect humility would be a full willingness, in all times and places, to find and do the will of God."

When I meditate upon such a vision, I need not be dismayed because I shall never attain it, nor need I swell with presumption that one of these days its virtues shall all be mine.

I only need to dwell on the vision itself, letting it grow and ever more fill my heart. This done, I can compare it with my last-taken personal inventory. Then I get a sane and healthy idea of where I actually stand on the Highway to Humility. I see that my journey toward God has scarce begun. As I thus get down to my right size and stature, my self-concern and importance become amusing. Then faith grows that I do have a place on this Highway; that I can advance upon it with deepening peace and confidence. Once more I know that God is good; that I need fear no evil. This is a great gift, this knowledge that I do have a destiny.

As I continue to contemplate God's perfection, I discover still another joy. As a child, hearing my first symphony, I was lifted up into its indescribable harmony, though I knew little of how or whence it came. So today, when I listen for God's music of the spheres, I can now and again hear those divine chords by which I am told that the great composer loves me — and that I love him.

LOVE

The Next Frontier:
Emotional Sobriety

January 1958

I think that many oldsters who have put our AA "booze cure" to severe but successful tests still find they often lack emotional sobriety. Perhaps they will be the spearhead for the next major development in AA — the development of much more real maturity and balance (which is to say, humility) in our relations with ourselves, with our fellows, and with God.

Those adolescent urges that so many of us have for top approval, perfect security, and perfect romance — urges quite appropriate to age seventeen — prove to be an impossible way of life when we are at age forty-seven or fifty-seven.

Since AA began, I've taken immense wallops in all these areas because of my failure to grow up, emotionally and spiritually. My God, how painful it is to keep demanding the impossible, and how very painful to discover finally, that all along we have had the cart before the horse! Then comes the final agony of seeing how awfully wrong we have been, but still finding ourselves unable to get off the emotional merry-go-round.

How to translate a right mental conviction into a right emotional result, and so into easy, happy, and good living — well, that's not only the neurotic's problem, it's the problem of life itself for all of us who have got to the point of real willingness to hew to right principles in all our affairs.

Even then, as we hew away, peace and joy may still elude us. That's the place so many of us AA oldsters have come to. And it's a hell of a spot, literally. How shall our unconscious — from which so many of our fears, compulsions, and phony aspirations still stream — be brought into line with what we actually believe, know, and want! How to convince our dumb, raging, and hidden "Mr. Hyde" becomes our main task.

I've recently come to believe that this can be achieved. I believe so because I begin to see many benighted ones — folks like you and me — commencing to get results. Last autumn, depression, having no really rational cause at all, almost took me to the cleaners. I began to be scared that I was in for another long chronic spell. Considering the grief I've had with depressions, it wasn't a bright prospect.

I kept asking myself, "Why can't the Twelve Steps work to release depression?" By the hour, I stared at the St. Francis Prayer . . . "It's better to comfort than to be the comforted." Here was the formula, all right. But why didn't it work?

Suddenly I realized what the matter was. My basic flaw had always been dependence — almost absolute dependence — on people or circumstances to supply me with prestige, security, and the like. Failing to get these things according to my perfectionist dreams and specifications, I had fought for them. And when defeat came, so did my depression.

There wasn't a chance of making the outgoing love of St. Francis a workable and joyous way of life until these fatal and almost absolute dependencies were cut away.

Because I had over the years undergone a little spiritual development, the *absolute* quality of these frightful dependencies had never before been so starkly revealed. Reinforced by what grace I could secure in prayer, I found I had to exert every ounce of will and action to cut off these faulty emotional dependencies upon people, upon AA, indeed, upon any set of circumstances whatsoever. Then only could I be free to love as Francis had. Emotional and instinctual satisfactions, I saw, were really the extra dividends of having love, offering love, and expressing a love appropriate to each relation of life.

Plainly, I could not avail myself of God's love until I was able to offer it back to him by loving others as he would have me. And I couldn't possibly do that so long as I was victimized by false dependencies.

For my dependency meant demand — a demand for the possession and control of the people and the conditions surrounding me.

While those words "absolute dependency" may look like a gimmick, they were the ones that helped to trigger my release into my present degree of stability and quietness of mind, qualities which I am now trying to consolidate by offering love to others regardless of the return to me.

This seems to be the primary healing circuit: an outgoing love of God's creation and his people, by means of which we avail ourselves of his love for us. It is most clear that

the real current can't flow until our paralyzing dependencies are broken, and broken at
depth. Only then can we possibly have a
glimmer of what adult love really is.

Spiritual calculus, you say? Not a bit of it.
Watch any AA of six months working with
a new Twelfth Step case. If the case says "To
the devil with you," the Twelfth Stepper only
smiles and turns to another case. He doesn't
feel frustrated or rejected. If his next case re-
sponds, and in turn starts to give love and at-
tention to other alcoholics, yet gives none
back to him, the sponsor is happy about it
anyway. He still doesn't feel rejected; instead
he rejoices that his one-time prospect is sober
and happy. And if his next following case
turns out in later time to be his best friend
(or romance), then the sponsor is most joy-
ful. But he well knows that his happiness is a
by-product — the extra dividend of giving
without any demand for a return.

The really stabilizing thing for him was
having and offering love to that strange

drunk on his doorstep. That was Francis at work, powerful and practical, minus dependency and minus demand.

In the first six months of my own sobriety, I worked hard with many alcoholics. Not a one responded. Yet this work kept me sober. It wasn't a question of those alcoholics giving me anything. My stability came out of trying to give, not out of demanding that I receive.

Thus I think it can work out with emotional sobriety. If we examine every disturbance we have, great or small, we will find at the root of it some unhealthy dependency and its consequent unhealthy demand. Let us, with God's help, continually surrender these hobbling demands. Then we can be set free to live and love; we may then be able to Twelfth Step ourselves and others into emotional sobriety.

Of course I haven't offered you a really new idea — only a gimmick that has started to unhook several of my own "hexes" at depth. Nowadays my brain no longer races compulsively in either elation, grandiosity, or depression. I have been given a quiet place in bright sunshine.

WHY ALCOHOLICS ANONYMOUS IS ANONYMOUS

January 1955

As never before the struggle for power, importance, and wealth is tearing civilization apart. Man against man, family against family, group against group, nation against nation.

Nearly all those engaged in this fierce competition declare that their aim is peace and justice for themselves, their neighbors, and their nations: Give us power and we shall have justice; give us fame and we shall set a great example; give us money and we shall be comfortable and happy. People throughout the world deeply believe that, and act accordingly. On this appalling dry bender, society seems to be staggering down a dead-end road. The stop sign is clearly marked. It says "Disaster."

What has this got to do with anonymity and Alcoholics Anonymous?

We of AA ought to know. Nearly every one of us has traversed this identical dead-end path. Powered by alcohol and self-justification, many of us have pursued the phantoms of self-importance and money right up to the disaster stop sign. Then came AA. We faced about and found ourselves on a new high road where the direction signs said never a word about power, fame, or wealth. The new signs read, "This way to sanity and serenity — the price is self-sacrifice."

Our new book, *Twelve Steps and Twelve Traditions*, states that "anonymity is the greatest protection our Society can ever have." It says also that "the spiritual substance of anonymity is sacrifice."

Let's turn to AA's twenty years of experience and see how we arrived at that belief, now expressed in our Traditions Eleven and Twelve.

At the beginning we sacrificed alcohol. We had to, or it would have killed us. But we couldn't get rid of alcohol unless we made other sacrifices. Big-shotism and phony thinking had to go. We had to toss self-justification, self-pity, and anger right out the window. We had to quit the crazy contest for personal prestige and big bank balances. We had to take personal responsibility for our sorry state and quit blaming others for it.

Were these sacrifices? Yes, they were. To gain enough humility and self-respect to stay alive at all we had to give up what had really been our dearest possession — our ambitions and our illegitimate pride.

But even this was not enough. Sacrifice had to go much further. Other people had to benefit too. So we took on some Twelfth Step work; we began to carry the AA message. We sacrificed time, energy, and our own money to do this. We couldn't keep what we had unless we gave it away.

Did we demand that our new prospects give us anything? Were we asking them for power over their lives, for fame for our good work, or for a cent of their money? No, we were not. We found that if we demanded any of these things our Twelfth Step work went flat. So these natural desires had to be sacrificed; otherwise, our prospects received little or no sobriety. Nor, indeed, did we.

Thus we learned that sacrifice had to bring a double benefit, or else little at all. We began to know about the kind of giving of ourselves that had no price tag on it.

When the first AA group took form, we soon learned a lot more of this. We found that each of us had to make willing sacrifices for the group itself, sacrifices for the common welfare. The group, in turn, found that it had to give up many of its own rights for the protection and welfare of each member, and for AA as a whole. These sacrifices had to be made or AA couldn't continue to exist.

Out of these experiences and realizations, the Twelve Traditions of Alcoholics Anonymous began to take shape and substance.

Gradually we saw that the unity, the effectiveness — yes, even the survival — of AA would always depend upon our continued willingness to sacrifice our personal ambitions and desires for the common safety and welfare. Just as sacrifice meant survival for the individual, so did sacrifice mean unity and survival for the group and for AA's entire Fellowship.

Viewed in this light, AA's Twelve Traditions are little else than a list of sacrifices which the experience of twenty years has taught us that we must make, individually and collectively, if AA itself is to stay alive and healthy.

In our Twelve Traditions we have set our

faces against nearly every trend in the outside world.

We have denied ourselves personal government, professionalism, and the right to say who our members shall be. We have abandoned do-goodism, reform, and paternalism. We refuse charitable money and prefer to pay our own way. We will cooperate with practically everybody, yet we decline to marry our Society to anyone. We abstain from public controversy and will not quarrel among ourselves about those things that so rip society asunder — religion, politics, and reform. We have but one purpose: to carry the AA message to the sick alcoholic who wants it.

We take these attitudes not at all because we claim special virtue or wisdom; we do these things because hard experience has told us that we must — if AA is to survive in the distraught world of today. We also give up rights and make sacrifices because we ought to — and, better yet, because we want to. AA is a power greater than any of us; it must go on living or else uncounted thousands of our kind will surely die. This we know.

Now where does anonymity fit into this picture? What is anonymity anyhow? Why do we think it is the greatest single protection that AA can ever have? Why is it our greatest symbol of personal sacrifice, the spiritual key to all our Traditions and to our whole way of life?

The following fragment of AA history will reveal, I deeply hope, the answer we all seek.

Years ago a noted ball player sobered up through AA. Because his comeback was so spectacular, he got a tremendous personal ovation in the press and Alcoholics Anonymous got much of the credit. His full name and picture, as a member of AA, were seen by millions of fans. It did us plenty of good; alcoholics flocked in. We loved this. I was specially excited because it gave me ideas.

Soon I was on the road, happily handing out personal interviews and pictures. To my delight, I found I could hit the front pages, just as he could. Besides, he couldn't hold his publicity pace, but I could hold mine. I only needed to keep traveling and talking. The local AA groups and newspapers did the rest. I was astonished when recently I looked at those old newspaper stories. For two or three years I guess I was AA's number one anonymity breaker.

So I can't blame any AA who has grabbed the spotlight since. I set the main example myself, years ago.

At the time, this looked like the thing to do. Thus justified, I ate it up. What a bang it gave me when I read those two-column spreads about "Bill the Broker," full name and picture, the guy who was saving drunks by the thousands!

Then this fair sky began to be a little overcast. Murmurs were heard from AA skeptics who said, "This guy Bill is hogging the big time. Dr. Bob isn't getting his share." Or, again, "Suppose all this publicity goes to Bill's head and he gets drunk on us?"

This stung. How could they persecute me when I was doing so much good? I told my critics that this was America and didn't they know I had the right of free speech? And wasn't this country and every other run by big-name leaders? Anonymity was maybe okay for the average AA. But co-founders ought to be exceptions. The public certainly had a right to know who *we* were.

Real AA power-drivers (prestige-hungry people, folks just like me) weren't long in catching on. They were going to be exceptions, too. They said that anonymity before the general public was just for timid people; all the braver and bolder souls, like themselves, should stand right up before the flash bulbs and be counted. This kind of courage would soon do away with the stigma on alcoholics. The public would right away see what fine citizens recovered drunks could make. So more and more members broke their anonymity, all for the good of AA. What if a drunk *was* photographed with the governor? Both he and the governor deserved the honor, didn't they? Thus we zoomed along, down the dead-end road!

The next anonymity-breaking development looked even rosier. A close AA friend of mine wanted to go in for alcohol education. A department of a great university interested in alcoholism wanted her to go out and tell the general public that alcoholics were sick people, and that plenty could be done about it. My friend was a crack public speaker and writer. Could she tell the general public that she was an AA member? Well, why not? By using the name Alcoholics Anonymous she'd get fine publicity for a good brand of alcohol education and for AA, too. I thought it an excellent idea and therefore gave my blessing.

AA was already getting to be a famous and valuable name. Backed by our name and her own great ability, the results were immediate. In nothing flat her own full name and picture, plus excellent accounts of her educational project, and of AA, landed in nearly every large paper in North America. The public understanding of alcoholism increased, the stigma on drunks lessened, and AA got new members. Surely there could be nothing wrong with that.

But there was. For the sake of this short-term benefit, we were taking on a future liability of huge and menacing proportions.

Presently an AA member began to publish a crusading magazine devoted to the cause of Prohibition. He thought Alcoholics Anonymous ought to help make the world bone dry. He disclosed himself as an AA member and freely used the AA name to attack the evils of whiskey and those who made it and drank it. He pointed out that he too was an "educator," and that his brand of education was the "right kind." As for putting AA into public controversy, he thought that was exactly where we should be. So he busily used AA's name to do just that. Of course, he broke his anonymity to help his cherished cause along.

This was followed by a proposal from a liquor trade association that an AA member take on a job of "education." People were to be told that too much alcohol was bad for anyone and that certain people — the alcoholics — shouldn't drink at all. What could be the matter with this?

The catch was that our AA friend had to break his anonymity; every piece of publicity and literature was to carry his full name as a member of Alcoholics Anonymous. This of course would be bound to create the definite public impression that AA favored "education," liquor-trade style.

Though these two developments never happened to get far, their implications were nevertheless terrific. They spelled it right out for us. By hiring out to another cause, and then declaring his AA membership to the whole public, it was in the power of an AA to marry Alcoholics Anonymous to practically any enterprise or controversy at all, good or bad. The more valuable the AA name became, the greater the temptation would be.

Further proof of this was not long in showing up. Another member started to put us into the advertising business. He had been commissioned by a life insurance company to deliver a series of twelve "lectures" on Alcoholics Anonymous over a national radio hookup. This would of course advertise life insurance and Alcoholics Anonymous — and naturally our friend himself — all in one good-looking package.

At AA Headquarters, we read the proposed lectures. They were about 50 percent AA and 50 percent our friend's personal religious convictions. This could create a false public view of us. Religious prejudice against AA would be aroused. So we objected.

Our friend shot back a hot letter saying that he felt "inspired" to give these lectures, and that we had no business to interfere with his right of free speech. Even though he was going to get a fee for his work, he had nothing in mind except the welfare of AA. And if we didn't know what was good for us, that was too bad! We and AA's board of trustees could go plumb to the devil. The lectures were going on the air.

This was a poser. Just by breaking anonymity and so using the AA name for his own purposes, our friend could take over our public relations, get us into religious trouble, put us into the advertising business and, for all these good works, the insurance company would pay him a handsome fee.

Did this mean that any misguided member could thus endanger our Society any time or any place simply by breaking anonymity and telling himself how much good he was going to do for us? We envisioned every AA advertising man looking up a commercial sponsor, using the AA name to sell everything from pretzels to prune juice.

Something had to be done. We wrote our friend that AA had a right of free speech too. We wouldn't oppose him publicly, but we could and would guarantee that his sponsor would receive several thousand letters of objection from AA members if the program went on the radio. Our friend abandoned the project.

But our anonymity dike continued to leak. AA members began to take us into politics. They began to tell state legislative committees — publicly, of course — just what AA wanted in the way of rehabilitation, money, and enlightened legislation.

Thus, by full name and often by pictures, some of us became lobbyists. Other members sat on benches with police court judges, advising which drunks in the lineup should go to AA and which to jail.

Then came money complications involving broken anonymity. By this time, most members felt we ought to stop soliciting funds publicly for AA purposes. But the educational enterprise of my university-sponsored friend had meanwhile mushroomed. She had a perfectly proper and legitimate need for money and plenty of it. Therefore, she asked the public for it, putting on drives to this end. Since she was an AA member and continued to say so, many contributors were confused. They thought AA was in the educational field or else they thought AA itself was raising money when indeed it was not and didn't want to.

So AA's name was used to solicit funds at the very moment we were trying to tell people that AA wanted no outside money.

Seeing what happened, my friend, wonderful member that she is, tried to resume her anonymity. Because she had been so thoroughly publicized, this has been a hard job. It has taken her years. But she has made the sacrifice, and I here want to record my deep thanks on behalf of us all.

This precedent set in motion all sorts of public solicitations by AAs for money — money for drying-out farms, Twelfth Step enterprises, AA boarding houses, clubs, and the like — powered largely by anonymity breaking.

We were next startled to learn that we had been drawn into partisan politics, this time for the benefit of a single individual. Running for public office, a member splashed his political advertising with the fact that he was an AA and, by inference, sober as a judge! AA being popular in his state, he thought it would help him win on election day.

Probably the best story in this class tells how the AA name was used to back up a libel lawsuit. A member, whose name and professional attainments are known on three continents, got hold of a letter which she thought damaged her professional reputation. She felt something should be done about this and so did her lawyer, also an AA. They assumed that both the public and AA would be rightfully angry if the facts were known. Forthwith, several newspapers headlined how Alcoholics Anonymous was rooting for one of its lady members — named in full, of course — to win her suit for libel. Shortly after this, a noted radio commentator told a listening audience, estimated at twelve million people, the same thing. This again proved that the AA name could be used for purely personal purposes — this time on a nationwide scale.

The old files at AA Headquarters reveal many scores of such experiences with broken anonymity. Most of them point up the same lessons.

They tell us that we alcoholics are the biggest rationalizers in the world; that fortified with the excuse we are doing great things for AA we can, through broken anonymity, resume our old and disastrous pursuit of personal power and prestige, public honors, and money — the same implacable urges that when frustrated once caused us to drink; the same forces that are today ripping the globe apart at its seams. Moreover, they make clear that enough spectacular anonymity breakers could someday carry our whole Society down into that ruinous dead end with them.

So we are certain that if such forces ever

rule our Fellowship, we will perish too, just as other societies have perished throughout human history. Let us not suppose for a moment that we recovered alcoholics are so much better or stronger than other folks; or that because in twenty years nothing has ever happened to AA, nothing ever can.

Our really great hope lies in the fact that our total experience, as alcoholics and as AA members, has at last taught us the immense power of these forces for self-destruction. These hard-won lessons have made us entirely willing to undertake every personal sacrifice necessary for the preservation of our treasured Fellowship.

This is why we see anonymity *at the general public level* as our chief protection against ourselves, the guardian of all our Traditions, and the greatest symbol of self-sacrifice that we know.

Of course, no AA need be anonymous to family, friends, or neighbors. Disclosure there is usually right and good. Nor is there any special danger when we speak at group or semi-public AA meetings, provided press reports reveal first names only.

But before the general public — press, radio, films, television, and the like — the revelation of full names and pictures is the point of peril. This is the main escape hatch for the fearful destructive forces that still lie latent in us all. Here the lid can and must stay down.

We now fully realize that 100 percent personal anonymity before the public is just as vital to the life of AA as 100 percent sobriety is to the life of each and every member. This is not the counsel of fear; it is the prudent voice of long experience. I am sure that we are going to listen; that we shall make every needed sacrifice. Indeed, we have been listening. Today only a handful of anonymity breakers remain.

I say all this with what earnestness I can; I say this because I know what the temptation of fame and money really is. I can say this because I was once a breaker of anonymity myself. I thank God that years ago the voice of experience and the urging of wise friends took me out of that perilous path into which I might have led our entire Society. Thus I learned that the temporary or seeming good can often be the deadly enemy of the permanent best. When it comes to survival for AA, nothing short of our very best will be good enough.

We want to maintain 100 percent anonymity for still another potent reason, one often overlooked. Instead of securing us more publicity, repeated self-serving anonymity breaks could severely damage the wonderful relation we now enjoy with press and public alike. We could wind up with a poor press and little public confidence at all.

For many years, news channels all over the world have showered AA with enthusiastic publicity, a never ending stream of it, far out of proportion to the news values involved. Editors tell us why this is. They give us extra space and time because their confidence in AA is complete. The very foundation of that high confidence is, they say, our continual insistence on personal anonymity at the press level.

Never before had news outlets and public relations experts heard of a society that absolutely refused personally to advertise its leaders or members. To them, this strange and refreshing novelty has always been proof positive that AA is on the square, that nobody has an angle.

This, they tell us, is the prime reason for their great goodwill. This is why, in season and out, they continue to carry the AA message of recovery to the whole world.

If, through enough anonymity lapses, we finally caused the press, the public, and our alcoholic prospects themselves to wonder about our motives, we'd surely lose this priceless asset; and, along with it, countless prospective members. Alcoholics Anonymous would not then be getting more good publicity; it would be getting less and worse. Therefore the handwriting on the wall is clear.

Because most of us can already see it, and because the rest of us soon will, I'm fully confident that no such dark day will ever fall upon our Society.

For a long time now, both Dr. Bob and I have done everything possible to maintain the Tradition of anonymity. Just before he died, some of Dr. Bob's friends suggested that there should be a suitable monument or mausoleum erected in honor of him and his wife, Anne, something befitting a founder. Dr. Bob declined, with thanks. Telling me about this a little later, he grinned and said, "For Heaven's sake, Bill, why don't you and I get buried like other folks?"

Last summer I visited the Akron cemetery where Bob and Anne lie. Their simple stone says never a word about Alcoholics Anonymous. This made me so glad I cried. Did this wonderful couple carry personal anonymity too far when they so firmly refused to use the words "Alcoholics Anonymous," even on their own burial stone?

For one, I don't think so. I think that this great and final example of self-effacement will prove of more permanent worth to AA than could any spectacular public notoriety or fine mausoleum.

We don't have to go to Akron, Ohio, to see Dr. Bob's memorial. Dr. Bob's real monument is visible throughout the length and breadth of AA. Let us look again at its true inscription — one word only, which we AAs have written. That word is sacrifice.

About Bill W.

Bill W. was born in East Dorset, Vermont, on November 26, 1895. With Dr. Bob S. of Akron, Ohio, he co-founded Alcoholics Anonymous in 1935. Hospitalized for alcoholism, he experienced a profound spiritual transformation that changed his life and inspired many of the principles of the AA movement.

Bill W. recognized that the recurring desire to drink disappears when one alcoholic works with another. This understanding became a basic principle of the new society. In addition, Bill promoted the idea that alcoholism is an illness, which can be arrested but not cured. Influenced by this AA concept, the American Medical Association later redefined alcoholism as a disease, not a failure of will.

AA's basic text, *Alcoholics Anonymous*, was written largely by Bill W. in association with other early AAs. Since its first publication in 1939, the Big Book, as it's called, has sold more than twenty-two million copies and has been translated into more than forty languages. The revolutionary Twelve-Step program of recovery it contains is the model for many other programs of recovery.

In the Twelve Traditions, first developed and presented in the pages of the Grapevine, Bill created a lasting blueprint for AA unity, incorporating the unique principles of anonymity, self-support, membership, and nonaffiliation.

In addition to his many writings, Bill devoted himself to developing an enduring service structure for Alcoholics Anonymous.

In June 1999, *Time* magazine named Bill W. as one of the hundred most influential people of the twentieth century.

He passed away on January 24, 1971.

The Twelve Steps

1. We admitted we were powerless over alcohol—that our lives had become unmanageable.

2. Came to believe that a Power greater than ourselves could restore us to sanity.

3. Made a decision to turn our will and our lives over to the care of God <u>as we understood Him.</u>

4. Made a searching and fearless moral inventory of ourselves.

5. Admitted to God, to ourselves, and to another human being the exact nature of our wrongs.

6. Were entirely ready to have God remove all these defects of character.

7. Humbly asked Him to remove our shortcomings.

8. Made a list of all persons we had harmed, and became willing to make amends to them all.

9. Made direct amends to such people wherever possible, except when to do so would injure them or others.

10. Continued to take personal inventory and when we were wrong promptly admitted it.

11. Sought through prayer and meditation to improve our conscious contact with God <u>as we understood Him</u>, praying only for knowledge of His will for us and the power to carry that out.

12. Having had a spiritual awakening as a result of these steps, we tried to carry this message to alcoholics, and to practice these principles in all our affairs.

The Twelve Traditions

1. Our common welfare should come first; personal recovery depends upon A.A. unity.

2. For our group purpose there is but one ultimate authority—a loving God as He may express Himself in our group conscience. Our leaders are but trusted servants; they do not govern.

3. The only requirement for A.A. membership is a desire to stop drinking.

4. Each group should be autonomous except in matters affecting other groups or A.A. as a whole.

5. Each group has but one primary purpose—to carry its message to the alcoholic who still suffers.

6. An A.A. group ought never endorse, finance, or lend the A.A. name to any related facility or outside enterprise, lest problems of money, property, and prestige divert us from our primary purpose.

7. Every A.A. group ought to be fully self-supporting, declining outside contributions.

8. Alcoholics Anonymous should remain forever nonprofessional, but our service centers may employ special workers.

9. A.A., as such, ought never be organized; but we may create service boards or committees directly responsible to those they serve.

10. Alcoholics Anonymous has no opinion on outside issues; hence the A.A. name ought never be drawn into public controversy.

11. Our public relations policy is based on attraction rather than promotion; we need always maintain personal anonymity at the level of press, radio, and films.

12. Anonymity is the spiritual foundation of all our traditions, ever reminding us to place principles before personalities.

Prayer of St. Francis

Lord, make me an instrument of thy peace.
Where there is hatred let me sow love
where there is injury, pardon
where there is doubt, faith
where there is despair, hope
where there is darkness, light
where there is sadness, joy.

O Divine Master grant that I
may not so much seek to be consoled
as to console; to be understood
as to understand; to be loved as to love.

For it is in giving that we receive;
it is in pardoning that we are pardoned
and it is in dying that we are born
to eternal life.